Dedicated to Zack and Finley, my two little dreamers.

Dreamy Dream Land

Tiny Tiger Publishing

Written by Sarah van Bakkum

At night time when Mommy puts me to bed,
After I'm bathed and fed,
I say night night, bye bye...

Then it's out of my room,
Just like a cartoon,
It's up up to the moon I fly!

I'll go dipping and diving through the houses.
Then over the roofs while watching my trousers.

Just look at me, free as could be.
Whooshing and swooshing, just like a bird.

Flapping and flopping, how absurd?

With my pillow so soft I gently drift off...
Zzzz

But sometimes when I´m dreaming,
I like to go beaming far up to Space,
Such a wonderful place,
And go walking on Mars, right next to the Stars.

Yes going to Space is really ace.
I'll cut to the chase, it's my favorite place.

Dream dream, time to dream.
It's off to Dream Land here I beam!

I don't need to pack a suitcase,
Or have to tie a shoe lace.

Don't need a giant coat,
Because in space I float!

But in a snippety snap,
I can be in a ....

. . . . . . Boat!

Dreamboat

I can sail the ocean and go floating around,
Hunting for treasure that's still to be found.

Jumping the decks, searching for wrecks,
And scaring off sharks, with big mighty barks!

Or I can go swimming deep in the Sea,
And meet my friend the Manatee.
He's really long, and very strong,
And loves to have a sing along.

I'll meet Gale the Whale,
Neil the Eel,
And Squishy the friendly Fishy.

You see...

Dreaming is such a pleasure,
you can really go wherever!

So sometimes I dream I go on a quest,
Searching for Lemurs far out West.

Swinging from trees, oh what a breeze,
Playing with monkeys and making them sneeze!

Aa-choo!

But sometimes I dream,
That I'm swimming downstream,
In a river made of yummy ice cream.

And sometimes I dream that I'm playing a Queen,
Wearing all green in a Hollywood movie scene.

You see...

When I go to sleep, I don't say a peep.
I close my eyes tight, and think what I like.

Then a few moments later,
I'm a fabulous skater,
Shouting "Yee Ha.. see ya later"

But there's only one problem,
It's not long enough.
When I wake up it's oh so tough!

"Just five more minutes that's all I need,
To finish my dream" I softly plead.

So you see...

Going to sleep is the best thing ever,
As you can really do whatever!

So tonight when you go to bed,
Where will you head?

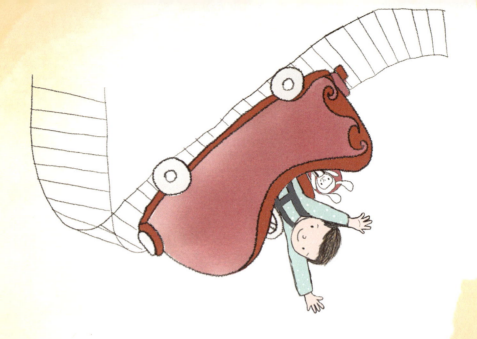

It's time to go.......

To Dreamy Dream Land!

Sarah Harvey

Is a writer from Liverpool, England who now lives in
Toronto, Canada. She developed a passion for writing children's
books after having her second son. Since then writing has become
her biggest passion. She has two boys, Zack and Finley, who are
the reason she started writing. They are the toughest critics.
Her aim is to write books that will inspire yet also entertain children.
Dreamy Dream Land is her first publication and there are another
two scheduled for publication in 2018 called The Spider Who Was
An Outsider and James and The Dragon Flames.

Ramona van Bakkum

Is an autodidact illustrator from The Netherlands.
She has been drawing since she was a child and always dreamed
of illustrating a children's book. Has three kids of her own who are
a big inspiration. She is also teaching schoolkids to draw.
To see more of Ramona's work go to: www.ramoon.nl